A NOTE FROM THE AUTHOR

For every tear, pain, trauma, and inward struggle, thank you. You have been my greatest teacher and the gift of God has been my greatest reward.

I wish I could take responsibility for the total of my life experiences, but that would create a false truth that I would never present to anyone. So, I say thank you, God, because You have been the solidarity and confidence that my life needs and requires.

just don't quit
PRISCILLA BOWENS VICTOR

A 21-DAY JOURNAL FOR THOSE WHO THINK THEY AREN'T GOOD ENOUGH

Just Don't Quit – 21 Day Journal
By Priscilla Bowens Victor

Cover Created by Jazzy Kitty Publications
Photography by BJ Shores courtesy of Shooterz Photoz
Logo Designs by Andre M. Saunders/Jess Zimmerman
Editor: Anelda L. Attaway

© 2020 Priscilla Bowens Victor
ISBN 978-1-954425-07-1

All rights reserved. This book is protected by the copyright laws of the United States of America. This book may not be copied or reprinted for commercial gain or profit. The use of short quotations or occasional page copying for personal or group study is permitted and encouraged. Permission will be granted upon request. This book is for Worldwide Distribution and printed in the United States of America, published by Jazzy Kitty Publications utilizing Microsoft Publishing Software. Scriptures are from the Holy Bible, KJV, NKJV, NIV, AMP versions. The "devil" is lowercased to honor God.

FORWARDS

This is an insightful, funny, and empowering daily conversation had with an awe-inspiring woman who has overcome so much and wants you to overcome too. From victory over the fear of pushing through, to God is a keeper of dreams. She is releasing so much positive energy and synergy you are destined to win. Take the journey with Priscilla, write your thoughts, formulate your vision, prepare to be challenged to go far beyond your limits, and change your mind. Know That your current place isn't the whole of your existence; there is yet much more for you to accomplish. This woman is a motivator and pusher to success. She will cause you to get away from those pigeons and find some eagles to soar with. She will help you fly! Your dreams can be a reality IF YOU JUST DON'T QUIT!

This woman is a bonafide and certified leader. Priscilla, I believe all your dreams are coming true!

Dr. Troy L. Davis Sr., Born 2 Lead, Coaching Specialist.

****

I am truly honored to forward this book "Just Don't Quit" I have worked with and watched Priscilla for about ten years. She has always been an overcomer and encourager to many. The love and sacrifice she has poured into other people's dreams are one of the reasons she is qualified to empower you not to quit.

Watching Priscilla maneuver through many personal and business adversity while never giving up is the biggest asset she has to offer you as you read this book. Her success and business adventures are tools that can be used to empower you to greatness.

This book is an adventure of unveiling and self-discovery into the secret place of success. The Principles and tools are designed to create self-motivation and discipline to propel you into destiny behaviors that transcend into destiny habits. Get ready to be challenged and changed for the better. If you read each chapter, be honest with yourself, and do the journal entries, you will begin to see on paper what you have learned or realized from the book has now taken shape and form to be executed in your life.

I believe this is now a destiny moment you are about to embark on. As you open yourself up to this life-changing experience, embrace it all. Get ready to be inspired to hold on, evaluate, and make a change.

Dr. Trina Davis, Coaching Specialist

DEDICATIONS

This book is dedicated to the people who are dearest to my heart:

First, to my husband, Gerry, and my three children, Gerry Jr., Ethan, and Geremiah.

Last but not least, both of my Grandmothers Mary and Stella who are strong and resilient.

Rest-in-Heaven

ACKNOWLEDGMENTS

First and foremost, I want to thank my Lord and Savior, Jesus Christ, who was patient with me and loved me even when I did not love myself.

To My Dear Husband, you have challenged me, encouraged me, inspired me even when I drove you crazy. Thank you for loving me and being patient with me, also for letting me create. I love you with all my heart & soul.

To My Boys, Gerry, Ethan, and Geremiah, you three inspire me; I know if I do these things, you will do even greater. You guys are my joy; Mommy loves you!

Mom & Dad, thank you for the greatest gift you ever gave me, first you for being my parents and second the knowledge of God – Jesus Christ. I am who I am because of you. Thank you for making me believe that I can do anything. I love you so much.

Bowens5...well, 4 – Parris, David, Lawrence, and Gregory, I couldn't ask for no better covering or love than from my brothers, you four, I love you. Thank you for always having my back and encouraging me in everything. I will love each of you forever.

My In-Loves Mom & Dad, thank you for your love, commitment to God, and your family. Thank you for always being there and loving me; I love you. I am a Victor, and I am so proud of that. Thank you for choosing me – My Honey-Luv.

My Sister-In-Loves (both sides), thank you for being real sisters. I don't have any biological sisters but being given the gift of your love reminds me that I never needed them because I have you all. I love you.

To My Tribe (My Sisters and my Sister-friends) Thank you for being genuine, honest, and holding me accountable. I treasure your friendship and I value your presence in my life. My sister-friends and daughters are the best. Thank you for being in my life.

TABLE OF CONTENTS

INTRODUCTION i
DAY 1 – Don't Fear 01
　Journal Entry #1 04
DAY 2 – Give Yourself Grace? 07
　Journal Entry #2 09
DAY 3 – Patience is Working on Me! 10
　Journal Entry #3 13
DAY 4 – Fight for It! 14
　Journal Entry #4 17
DAY 5 – Stronger 18
　Journal Entry #5 20
DAY 6 – Pressure 21
　Journal Entry #6 24
DAY 7 – Help! It's Complicated 25
　Journal Entry #7 27
DAY 8 – Push Through 28
DAY 9 – I've Got Goals 30
DAY 10 – "Now What?" 32
　Journal Entry #10 34
DAY 11 – Freedom is Yours! 35
　Journal Entry #11 38

TABLE OF CONTENTS

DAY 12 – Create Yourself!!! 40
    Journal Entry #12 42
DAY 13 – Distractions 43
    Journal Entry #13 45
DAY 14 – Protect Your Space.. 46
    Journal Entry #14 49
DAY 15 – Covenants – Friend or Foe?.................................. 20
    Journal Entry #15 50
DAY 16 – A Lil More Courage, Please 55
    Journal Entry #16 58
DAY 17 – Misunderstood! 59
    Journal Entry #17 62
DAY 18 – God is the Keeper of the Dream 64
DAY 19 – Write for Your Life 66
    Journal Entry #19 68
DAY 20 – Make Manifest 69
    Journal Entry #20 71
DAY 21 – The Finisher 72
    Journal Entry #21 74
ABOUT THE AUTHOR 76

INTRODUCTION

This journal is for every person who ever questioned were they good enough to achieve their dreams and goals.

It's for those who see the vision and can taste, know that it's time to acquire it, and then to walk in it.

It's for those who have stopped and started more times than they've cared to admit. I say Just Don't Quit…there is more.

I remember feeling less than and not worthy of being used by God or anyone else. But I knew I had big dreams, at least they were big to me. This book is a dream, a vision and a goal fulfilled…because I didn't quit.

DAY 1

DON'T FEAR

Hey, Yawwwwwl...Ok, so it's day 1, the beginning of a thing, right. If your anything like me, you have started many things and a great deal of those things remain unfinished. How so, you say? Because life is so crazy and so much is always happening, right? Nope, not so right for me; I was scared! Scared that the things I began were too big or bound for success. How crazy does that sound? I was afraid it might work or that it was going to definitely work? Another truth is that I was terrified that it might work and might be amazing, but who else really would believe in my dream? After all, I'm just a girl from North Philly. I mean, I played the minimizer game and found ten thousand reasons why no one could want to hear anything I had to say or less see what I would create. Self-doubt is a doozy! Fear sucks, and anxiety is the devil--Tee Hee Hee.

Let me get back on track.

As I have had so many life experiences, I have become exhausted with fear at this tender age. I put on my socks and suit and ran to court and had an emotional divorce with fear, the judge on the one hand, and myself on the other.

The judge asked me why am I making such a hard request? I mean, divorce is so final. And I emotionally, with tears in my eyes, screamed yes! Absolutely! I am tired of being afraid. I'm sick of the nervous and bubbly stomach; sorry for the visual pic drawn. But I was exhausted, and I needed freedom from the what-ifs.

"I mean, God, is this really what You meant for me? Like God, You truly give me all of these desires and assume that I could pull it off and then send a little helper call fear. I mean...Seriously!

And in true God fashion, He was like, "Naw, that wasn't me." I know, I know, but these are how the conversations happen in my head.

Fear is not a Godly quality, principle, or gift. God tells us not to fear because He is with us. Like WOW, what if we just believed His word.

"Well, Your Honor, I believe God's word, and it's time for fear and me to part ways. I'm leaving with everything I came with, hopes, dreams, and callings. The case of fear has been closed over my life. I trust God, and I fear no more."

We do not have space in our heads, hearts, or lives for fear. There are so many amazing and wonderful things that God desires to give to us, and we have to believe only God and run for it. Take a chance at it and give it a 100% try. God would not give us a vision or a dream and a desire just for us not to obtain it. If it's there, it means it's for us to do. So, I admonish you to do like I did and ask yourself a few questions. Then start the proceedings to your fear of divorce because you deserve every desire, hope, and dream God has implanted in your heart.

PRAYER TO REMOVE FEAR

"God, I ask that You light a fire of hope and dreams into the lives of the reader. I ask that You speak into their hearts, minds, and secret places where they are scared to go and show them exactly what You have for them. In a real way, God let them feel Your presence and let them feel that You will strengthen and help them with Your righteous hand. We believe that Your word is true, and we will do everything You have set before. In Jesus' Name. Amen."

Journal Entry #1

Write the dream, the hope, and what scares you most.

Write your breakup letter to fear.

Pick a scripture to remind you that you can carry along as a reminder.

_____

_____

_____

_____

_____

_____

Come back to this to remind yourself when you feel fear that God is with you!

_____

_____

_____

_____

_____

_____

_____

_____

DAY 2

GIVE YOURSELF GRACE

Welcome back for some more; more of what you say, encouragement, love, and fight. That's right; I am fighting for you. I am fighting for every single person who will read this. I believe that it helps to know that someone is over here, pulling for you and in the fight with you. I need to see everyone win.

There are so many times that we feel like our journey is the total of who we are, and we do not allow ourselves to grow and mature. We mostly keep the sins and bad decisions we've made before us, and we let it shape us like we are clay on the potter's wheel. GIVE YOURSELF GRACE. We are not our experiences. We are not the things that have happened to us. Those experiences have made us the powerful people that we are. I praise God for every failure and learning experience because, without them, I would have no journal to write and no encouragement to give. It is my pleasure and good joy to remind you of how amazing you are. It is my duty as your sister-friend to let you know that you are brought here to this life to live on purpose. God is not a joke; those who make it out of the womb are truly called here to fulfill purpose in the earth. With that being said, GIVE YOURSELF GRACE!

It is Ok to be weary and tired after all that we face in our daily lives; I don't blame you. I even give you space to be in your moment, and yes, I say moment because it shouldn't last long at all. We have to learn to pull ourselves out of that weary place. I know this place all too well. It's very comfortable, like a snugly blanket that knows all of our problems. We can't let weary or tired run our lives. Give in to the moment, get some sleep so that you can recharge and run again. The runner must be dedicated to the race. You being the runner, take the breaks when you need them but continue to train for the main event. Go, fight, and run the event. Rest and Recharge! Do it again.

When things do not come out the way we would desire them to, just continue to gradual steps in the direction you desire, and you will get to your destination. Consistency is key.

Journal Entry #2

1) What areas of your life can you use a little more grace?

_____
_____
_____
_____
_____

2) What does grace look like for you?

_____
_____
_____
_____
_____

3) Write three affirmations you can repeat when you find yourself lacking grace?

_____
_____
_____
_____
_____

***Don't forget that you owe yourself the grace to grow, change, and correct-you should give it yourself. ***

DAY 3

PATIENCE IS WORKING ON ME!

Some days, I just don't have it. Some days life is just a little overbearing. I am not patient with myself, patient with others, or even patient with God. Right, the nerve of me, not patient with God. But if you are honest, we usually asked God for something and expect an immediate answer. Sometimes the answer is yes, no, or not yet, and most of us hate the not yet answer. Or the long journey to a yes. It's the same frustration we see with our selves.

How many times have you been less patient with yourself? I am most impatient with myself because I do not exceed my expectations, and when I don't get my choices right. The worst thing I am impatient about is seeing the evidence of growth within myself. It's almost like I'd say I'll quit overworking, but I'm first in line as soon as overtime is offered. Or let discuss food; yes, I said that good ole sweet potato cheesecake is necessary. Except when trying to lose pounds, but who can refuse? Oh no, not me, I'm going to eat all of it. Please, but by the end of that day, the guilt that sets in is ridiculous, funny, right? I know, I know that's pie. But life gets you wrapped up in it like that. The goals and dreams you pressed for seeming so far away. The hard work and sleepless nights don't add up yet; it's working on your patience.

Guess what, friends, we aren't patient with others either. We often run out of chances with other people. We don't often have the patience for the difference in other people. What I mean by this, we expect people to act like us, think like us, and do what we would do. Except, they aren't us. Their perspective is their own and we have to allow patience for people to walk out. They're our viewpoint. It can be frustrating to have people around who do not think like you. Some may even feel that the relationship is counterproductive. It is not; it's the beauty of individuality and a gift from God. We must have patience with others because we miss the beauty of great relationships when we lose patience with others. Let patience keep working you in this area; you will be grateful down the line.

Lastly, let's have patience with God; as crazy as it sounds, it's true. Have you ever asked God for anything and then did not receive it when you thought you were due to get it. It's like we become little children; we have temper-tantrums, running around our lives mad, screaming, "Why can't I have that husband, job, car, house, and promotion?" We just out here having a great big attitude instead of trusting God. When we ask God for something and don't get an answer, we can't fathom that God would leave us hanging. When, in fact, God never leaves us without exactly what we need. I found that His answer goes something like yes, no, or not yet. It's the not yet one that grinds my gears. It's because I don't know what yet is; I'm not sure if that means next week, next month, next year, I mean the next generation. The not yet is hard. I call that patience having its work on me. I reserve the right to say when God and patience are through working on you and with you, you will be perfect and want nothing.

When we are patient, we learn so much about ourselves, the people in our lives, and God. Life is teaching us even though we may not be receptive. Let's become open to the lessons God is trying to teach us. If we are honest with ourselves, a lot of God withholding somethings are for our protection. It does not feel that way at the moment. But take a look back and see where God said no and not yet, and good, great, thank you should cross your lips. Thank you, Lord!

Journal Entry #3

1) What is your definition of patience?
_____
_____
_____

2) Write a small quick prayer for you to say when you find yourself overwhelmed?
_____
_____
_____

3) List the areas that you find yourself exhibiting less patience.
_____
_____
_____

4) Write how you can extend patience in that area in order to grow.
_____
_____
_____

Patience is the key to growth, be patient with yourself!

DAY 4

FIGHT FOR IT!

YOU MUST FIGHT!!! Now, wait just one second, put your hands down, and get on your knees. Prayer & Praise is your greatest weapon. They are not for the weak and scary; they are for those who want to win the fight. Now is not the time to quit or walk away. What is it that you love? What have you been called to? What is the vision and purpose for your life? What vision or dream keeps reoccurring in your heart mind and even comes through your sleep? FIGHT FOR IT!!!! That's it, your vision, and it is worth fighting for.

I wrote this journal because I am a person with so many dreams and visions. I would become frustrated because I'm like, God, why would you give me all of this? What am I supposed to do with it? I used to become intimidated because other people were qualified and doing the same I was doing. So, I wouldn't even try, or I would quit in the middle. How dumb. I had to get tired of seeing the same dreams and visions come back repeatedly. The visions and dreams of my life are so before me these days; I cannot outrun them. I have to do everything. God gave me these talents, and I cannot bury them in the sand and act as if they don't exist. God wants a return on his investment in my life. So, the dreams will always come. Fear was my greatest hindrance; I was so afraid that people would see me, and they would know I'm not perfect or nothing would be perfect, and everything would crumble. I would be over inundated with the idea that my experiences were not enough to share or help anyone else. How foolish. Self-talk is a monster, and just like we talk ourselves into these horrible thoughts, we have to talk ourselves out of it. SO, I FIGHT for the dreams and visions God has given me!!!

- What are you fighting for?
- What has God given you?
- What is your heart's desire?
- What are you holding on to? Is there any life in it?

Here are three things you must fight for before anything else:

1. Your relationship with God
2. Yourself
3. Your Vision/Dream

Your relationship with God is worth fighting for, period! I'm a witness that there was a time in my life that I let the circumstances in my life make me pull back from my relationship with God. I felt that to maintain this relationship; I had to not be so much in a relationship with God. I found myself to be totally miserable. It was the biggest fight of my life to get back to God and the life-sustaining relationship for me. I promise I will never let a soul come between God and me. GOD FIRST...ME NEXT! YOU are worth fighting for...Period!

Just like my God relationship went out the window, so do my love for me. I put everything in front of myself. I answered and catered to everyone's needs before my own. The truth of the matter is how helpful am I to anyone if I don't take care of myself first. I am done with that. I put myself second.

Your DREAMS are worth fighting for. Do I need to say it again? God trusted you with a load of gifts; they are often called dreams. It calls you when your sleep and tugs at you when you awake. It's that thing that won't leave that only you can do because God placed it in your heart and you are responsible for giving that dream back to God. You won't rest until to tend to the dream.

So, fight for with all your heart, soul, and mind. God will teach you how to fight. You must pray and ask the Lord to teach you how to fight for God, yourself, and your dreams. YOU ARE WORTH FIGHTING FOR!

Journal Entry #4

1) Write about a situation where you wanted to fight for yourself, but you didn't?

_____
_____
_____

2) What would you have done differently?

_____
_____
_____

3) What makes you want to fight for it now?

_____
_____
_____

4) How will you fight for yourself in the future?

_____
_____
_____

Don't forget: You are worth fighting for; your dreams are worth fighting for & your vision is worth fighting for.

DAY 5

STRONGER

Friend, my prayer is that you become stronger and that your experiences do not make you bitter but more powerful. My prayer is that you become emotionally, mentally, and physically stronger. Sometimes, life can knock us around so much that we just want to give up. Please don't give up, don't quit; we build muscle with all the ups and downs. We are becoming stronger, we are building our faith, and we are trusting in God. The trials that terrorize our lives are only here to make us strong. I am only able to be a witness to strength because of my experiences. The only way we can push through to the other side is to build strength. This means, at times when we want to run and cry, we must stand and fight. We must stand on the word and truth of God and use His strength, even when we are weak.

The Bible says, *"For my strength is made perfect in weakness."* 2 Cor. 9.

God's strength is more than enough when we are weak, afraid, or unsure. God's strength is enough when we don't see the other side, or even when we don't have enough faith in knowing that God is in control. Borrow the strength of God, and you will find yourself to be stronger as the days grow. Trust in the Lord, believe in Him, and call upon the Lord for His strength, and you'll be stronger.

Your God muscles will have no fear of fighting off the things that come your way because God will be with you. This is the promise of God. Have faith in God, Trust in God for His strength is made perfect in your weakness. Where is it that you need strength today?

Journal Entry #5

1) List three times in your life where you felt weak based on your situation?

_____

_____

_____

2) How could you have built or gained strength form these experiences?

_____

_____

_____

3) Create three affirmations to draw strength from in weal moments:

_____

_____

_____

4) How will you fight for yourself in the future?

_____

_____

_____

Know that the only way to build strength is by exercising the muscle; the muscle here is you! Exercise your life.

DAY 6

PRESSURE

Life is so funny; as much as we think we are in control and have all of our stuff together, it just isn't true. We plan our days, make our schedules, everything is set to the drop, and we know what will happen next. And before we could even get full into the plan, it call goes to shambles. It will start with one small thing going wrong, and then another and another. It seemingly turns right into a snowball effect. You begin to see the pressure mount and feel the adversity closing in. If you are anything like me, you're praying for a small stick pen to let some of the air out slowly, but it usually goes nowhere. PRESSURE!!! That's what you feel.

I know for myself pressure was always thought of as a bad thing. I would literally run or quit as soon as it presented itself. I have learned over time that pressure builds. I know, crazy right, but think of yourself as a pearl, you're in a tight space, and the pressures, which are the sands of life, are squeezing you, irritating you, and rubbing you all the wrong way. You are sick and tired, but once enough pressure has been built, the shell opens, and you are presented as a beautiful treasure. Nothing beautiful happens without pressure being applied. We must learn how to adjust when the pressure closes in. We learn this by going to the one who created us.

When I find pressure closing in on me, and I can't get any answers to my questions, my feelings are cloudy, and I simply shut down. When pressure is applied to quiet myself and take (yes, aggressively), I have learned to take space to be yourself and be quiet. When I take this space, I am usually listening to worship music, I am taking a long walk, and mostly I am praying and crying. I say the word "TAKE" aggressively because we do so much, and if you don't take the space and time it will take you, and the pressure will overtake you. During this time of prayer and space, I cry a lot because I am unloading to God what is on me, and usually, uncertainty does not feel good and renders me vulnerable. I don't like that feeling. It makes me feel weak sometimes, and I know for a fact after everything I've been through, I am not weak. But those pressure-filled moments may knock the wind out of me. The peace of God will quiet your soul and cause you to make the right decisions. You will then swing pressure in the right direction outward and not let it build in you.

Friend, ask God, what is this pressure building at this

moment? Ask God, is there something going on inside me that is making this issue or thought a pressurized time? God, what is your plan for all of this that is on my plate?

Journal Entry #6

1) What is building the pressure in your life, what is it?

_____

_____

_____

2) What was the previous issues that were dwelling in your heart prior to this issue?

_____

_____

_____

3) Take each issue, write them, and separate them. This will allow you to look at each thing separately and write a different solution.

_____

_____

_____

4) How will you fight for yourself in the future?

_____

_____

_____

Know that the only way to build strength is by exercising the muscle; the muscle here is you! Exercise your life.

DAY 7

HELP! IT'S COMPLICATED...

Life has a way of bringing you to a place called done. There are so many things that draw you to this kind of place. It's usually a bunch of things that are happening all at once, which means you have to make a decision. Now, the complicated I'm speaking about is not your basic Ok, so blue shirt today or orange shirt. It's not fish or chicken. It's not pumps or boots. It's, do I work at this job, do I go to this school? Do I buy this house? Do I start this business? What's going on with my children? Is it the school? The sitter? Friends? It's the things that are troubling you and causing you sleepless nights.

If we are honest with ourselves, we will see that all of these thoughts and or situations produce thoughts in our minds. If your anything like me, then it's a negative thought that usually enters my mind. And it consumes me like a rushing tide coming to take me out to the ocean. And I can't get out. that's usually when I'm yelling, "HELLLLLLLPPPPPPPP." Because there's no yes or no answer, it's usually an if and a then.

I run to the Lord for refuge; I go to God for strength; I trust

Him! I have confidence, faith, and full reliance on His power to steer me in the right direction. When my inner me is unsafe, I know that God is my refuge, and I can go to Him and hide.

PRAYER

"Father God, help us today, silence the voices. Silence the fear and doubt that invades our hearts. God, I ask that You would rid us of the guilt or shame that comes when thinking of our past choices. Father God, we ask You to hold us together and grant us peace to do Your will. As we make these next great decisions, I ask that You study our hearts and minds and guide us along the way.

We love You, Lord. In Jesus' Name Amen."

Journal Entry #7

1) What is complicating your life? Writing it may help you see it from a different perspective.

_____
_____
_____
_____
_____

2) What will it take for you to give it to God?

_____
_____
_____
_____
_____

3) Using wisdom and a sound mind how will you move forward with your decisions.

_____
_____
_____
_____
_____

Remember that God is your Refuge - Trust Him!

DAY 8

PUSH THROUGH

We know what to do, we know how to do it, we start it, but we don't finish it. Why? Where is the PUSH THROUGH? Where is the part that says see it through? When you have a dream or a vision, sometimes in building the dream, you hit a plateau. When hitting that plateau, it sometimes can discourage you from walking the vision out. But my friend, the course is yours to take, and you must PUSH THROUGH. Push it into overdrive, into kill mode, and make it happen.

JUST DONT QUIT!!! Don't get weary I know it seems bleak and that what you set out to accomplish won't come to past-it will. You were designed for your task at hand. You were created and made for this calling. People are waiting for you and need you to PUSH THROUGH to the other side so that you can reach those who you were born to reach. There is a little girl or boy out there who saw you during your grind and said that you were the mark they were pressing toward. You are the person that inspired them. You are the reason they think they can do anything. What about your daughter, son, nieces, and nephews? What about your sister and brother and even your mother and father? The drive and push that you have will directly affect those who are close to you. Your success is shared and so is your failure. Don't Quit.

Friend, you got this, don't get weary; you are doing well, you will reap well.

Don't get weary - PUSH Through

DAY 9

I GOT GOALS

Goals, goals, goals...how many of us have them? We all do, whether they be short-term, long-term...large goals, or small goals. We have something that we desire to do and we hope that we are complete with them. It is the heart of God for us to have dreams and visions to fulfill purpose in the earth-so let's get to it. What do you daydream about? What's something you would do forever, even if you never received payment for it? What have you written down that you have not started the process on? What have you been saying to yourself, "If I weren't working, I would...?"

That's the goal!

The Bible says, in Habakkuk 2:2, *"And the LORD answered me: "Write the vision; make it plain on tablets, so he may run who reads it."* This is a clear statement, and I believe in it based on what I have experienced in my life. I have hundreds of journals where I have written my hopes and dreams; I have seen them come to pass. There is power and prophecy in writing;

you will have what you say...TRUST ME! No trust the Lord, He said write it.

So here are some ways that I approach writing things:

1) List everything that comes to mind - just jot it all down.

2) Write it Out - Got to each thing you've written down and further explain how you see it. Now, this part may take time because it needs to be explained. So, take as long as it needs to be done.

3) Map it out - take a blank paper, write the project your working on in the middle, draw a circle around it, and draw a line from it, and write different parts of the vision for that project. Hey, you can cut out pictures and put them on a board so that it's 3D and alive. Color brings the vision alive too. You can do this with each project that you desire to do.

Friends get it down...WRITE ITTTTTTT!!!!!

That's the journal entry...Start writing...Hurry up, get to it!

WE'VE GOT GOALS

I am so excited for you and this part of the journal because it's a fresh start and an opportunity to dream and love it.

GET TO WRITING!!!

DAY 10

"NOW WHAT?"

Do it! That's what! Let's do it...sometimes we get scared of what we wrote down and it looks bigger than us once we really dive into it! But you can do it! You are amazing and powerful and able to do exactly what you saw. God would not have given you the vision and the ability to write it out and not help make it so. You! Yes, you are the one to do it. Trust God! He will open every door as you get to it.

Don't listen to your self-talk because that will slow you down. Just do it! I feel like as I reach goals and do what I'm destined to do, I am closer to God. Maybe you've felt that way. But, when I know I'm doing something my heart and soul is longing to do, it goes straight to the heart of God, and I feel a relief that I got it done. And then, like clockwork, God shows me something else to do next.

Listen, you are wonderful and fearfully created with so much potential and richness within you, and the world needs access to your gifts. Remember gifts are meant to be given and just one gift rendered from you can save someone's life. Get to it. Write the book, the play, make the video, produce the movie, paint the picture, start the non-profit, began the LLC, start the business. Hey friend, I'm not done...cook the food, share the call, make the clothes, create the thirsts, start the restaurant, or go back to school. Whatever, you find your hands, heart, soul, and mind to do...DO it!!! It is the destiny for your life. It will blow your mind.

What's stopping you...? What's holding you back? What's stopping you? You need to know what it is so that you can get past it. The reality is that nothing is holding us back but us. We get in our own way so bad, all of the what-ifs slow us down. We do better just to start, one foot in front of the other.

I challenge you to start...and God will layout and lead you to the next.

Journal Entry #10

1) Have you begin working on the goal yet? Why or why not?

_____
_____
_____
_____

2) What is some of your apprehensions? What is troubling you about it?

_____
_____
_____
_____

Activity Alert: Look in the mirror as confessing these words:
- -I will finish what I started!
- -I can do this; nothing is too hard for God.
- -These challenges are helping me to grow.
- -I will never give up.
- -I AM GOOD ENOUGH!
- -I will finish what I started!

You got this...Now go Do it!

DAY 11

FREEDOM IS YOURS!

There is a peace that guides us into freedom. This is the same peace that lets us know we are in the right space at the right time of our lives. This is a wave of peace once received that we do not lose, but we guard safely so that we can be FREE!

Daily we go through our everyday lives and we have some tough experiences, but freedom is available. God has a call on your life, so we cannot let the things of the world sway us from our God-given calling because when we do…freedom just doesn't seem free anymore. I remember a time when I used to describe my life as a prison. I felt so much judgment and scrutiny for basic things I felt like I could not be myself, and everything that I wanted and desired would never be reached because I allowed myself to be in the situation I was in. If I am completely honest with myself…I was ashamed and guilty of the state that your life was in, and I felt trapped inside of my own world. But God!

I had to quiet myself and submit myself to God. I had to

pray for days and seek God's face for that still small voice that leads us and guides us into the correct things for our lives. In doing this, I begin to hear God speak and give me directions. During this time, God was on me about forgiveness. I did not realize that I was harboring unforgiveness for the people that were around me every day and whom I loved with all my heart. It caused me to shut down, become reserve and reclused, and I started building an emotional shell. Why? Because when you are hurt, you don't want to feel. But I didn't realize that the shell I built to keep others out locked me in...Whew! Now that was a word! Listen, I thought what I was doing healthy, and boy was I wrong. I started the journey of forgiving and changing my behavior, showing love despite the hurt. I started showed love even when it hurt until it did not hurt. I kept reading the word and praying and getting that word in my heart. I hid the word in my heart so that it would become the bank of love that I operated from. As I did my part forgiving and letting go, I forgave them, and God forgave me. As well, the friendship and relationship are Christ-centered and so much better. I also let go of the shame, the guilt, and the hurt; I am now so free. I mean free to the point that all of those feelings I had of feeling trapped does not even exist. The interesting thing is that I built that reality for myself. I saw for myself that when things go wrong in our lives, we build a reality for us, which may not be true. We have to fight that and build the lives and mindset that God has for us because freedom belongs to us.

The Bible says, *"And the peace of God [that peace which reassures the heart, that peace] which transcends all understanding, [that peace which] stands guard over your hearts and your minds in Christ Jesus [is yours]."* Phil 4:7 (AMP) This scripture is the business you in when you trust the Lord and give it all to Him. Freedom becomes yours, the peace of God transcends through your life, and it changes you forever.

Journal Entry #11

1) What has you locked up in your emotions?
_____
_____
_____
_____

2) Have you forgiven those people you need to forgive? Write it down. (Even something small because those feeling usually grows.)
_____
_____
_____
_____

3) Pull three scriptures that you can use on forgiveness and healing daily...
_____
_____
_____
_____
_____

Take this time to pray and talk to God about it, ask for forgiveness for your unforgiveness. You may also need to do this until your heart is clear, and it doesn't hurt anymore.

Friend, God has got you; He wants you to live free and abundantly.

DAY 12

CELEBRATE YOURSELF!!!

You are worthy of celebration, just your existence and the fact that you're pushing through against all odds. We all have come from somewhere and experienced so many different things that have shaped our lives and our choices. You are so awesome and amazing because in spite of the challenges that you faced, you survived.

We often minimize our experiences because we chalk it up as unimportant. Just keep in mind that if someone else had taken your steps, it would have killed them. Please don't consider waking up every morning as a small thing. God is infinite in his wisdom is sovereign. He does not prep us or tells us what we will face to arrive at a place of surrender. I can tell, though, that if you make it to that place, you will know that you have survived and that God is King.

Some of you have survived abuse, drugs, depression, fear, and self-doubt. All of the above things together and collectively can take you out. Sometimes you just have to stop and celebrate. When you on the road to your destination, it could be mundane and hard, so break it up, stop, and dance. Write down what you have accomplished and celebrate yourself. Celebrate progress, celebrate the steps, celebrate the failures, and keep going.

This is a short chapter because the point is the truth. Celebrate it all. Thank God for it all. Because anyone else could be in your space, but you are the chosen one for this journey. Take the time to write during your journey so that you never for the press and struggle to keep you grounded. It will also help you remember where you came from so that you don't lose yourself in the process.

I celebrate you; you are one amazing person. There is no other person like you. You were created in the image and love of God. You are worthy of love, peace, and joy. Just know that you are loved and will forever be celebrated by...ME!

Journal Entry #12

Make a List - This is for you to affirm yourself and remind yourself of your accomplishments, things you are grateful for, and the things you hope to accomplish. Make a list when you start to doubt, go back, and read the list again.

_____
_____
_____
_____
_____
_____
_____
_____
_____
_____
_____
_____
_____
_____

Re-read that list over and over again until you are overtaken with joy.

DAY 13

DISTRACTIONS!!!

The Oxford Dictionary says that the word distraction means "a thing that prevents someone from giving full attention to something." Wow! Seriously though. And that's the end of this chapter.

We are distracted a lot of times with the things of life and our daily coming and goings. It's these things that usually get us off course and prevents us from finishing what we've started. It's the devil's cardinal plan to distract us so that we do not fulfill God's purpose for our lives on the earth. We are usually distracted by different things; sometimes it's things that we like, there are often we are distracted with trauma and pain. It comes and sideswipe us and takes our breath away. When these things happen, some people never recover. Others lose time trying to simply get back to where they were before. Others fight like there is no tomorrow to get past it and on to purpose. Which one are you? Are you still lost in the sideswiped lane? Has it's been years and you haven't found your way back to yourself, are you just lost? Has it been five years since your heartbreak, and you are stuck in the quicksand of the whys, and why me? Will I ever love again? Or are you fighting and pushing past depression, trauma, and self-doubt? All you want to do is receive your healing and ultimately fulfill your purpose in the earth? Take a minute and think about which one you are.

I know, I just threw it all out there and rather abruptly, pretty much how life throws things at us. Please hang in and don't quit. It will get better; your vision will get clearer, and the life that seems useless you will find is so much bigger than what you're facing. Take heart and be encouraged; those things that tried to hold you back can't win. You are in a war with no one; you are competing in life with no one. All you have to do is reach for the goals that God has set for you.

And know as it says in the Bible, *"If God is for you who can be against you."*

(Romans 8:31) Think of it like this, you're standing there, but when others look at you, they see a huge giant standing behind you. And along as that giant (God) is right there by your side, there is no doubt, hate, depression, hopelessness, or dreams deferred can do nothing to stop you. The only thing it does is distract you. Your purpose and vision still have to be fulfilled in the earth. And it will.

Journal Entry #13

Make a List - This is for you to affirm yourself and remind yourself of your accomplishments, things you are grateful for, and the things you hope to accomplish. Make a list; when you start to doubt, go back, and reread the list.

What distractions are you facing right now? List them:

_____

_____

_____

_____

What mantras or confirmations can you write to remind yourself to get rid of distractions.

Here is mine: "Starve your distractions & Feed your Focus" - Author Unknown

Write Your below:

_____

_____

_____

"Father, I ask that You rid my friends of the distractions that are costing them time, pain, and money. I ask that You will place a divine focus on their lives and propel them into the next phases of their lives and into completion. I believe it's done. In Jesus' Name, Amen."

DAY 14

PROTECT YOUR SPACE

Have you ever been in a room full of people and felt that the walls were closing in on you. Then you go into a room of people where you feel safe, warm, and protected and feel home? Yup, we have all felt like we didn't belong in a room and sometimes unwanted in the room. Do I leave it, or do I embrace it and see what I can learn about myself in that room.

When I am writing, painting, sewing, or just creating, it has to be in an environment where I feel safe, or I cannot create. It's the weirdest thing, almost as if my thoughts are saying, this space is no good for your intellectual ability. I know I know I'm being deep. but space is important. There are a few kinds of space that I have noticed:

1. The space around me globally - the world
2. The space beside me - room/home
3. The space inside of me

The space around me:

The world is your oyster, they say, but why are people being murdered unjustly? Why are they hungry? Why is there such negativity and brutality? I mean, yes, there is good, but sometimes the evil of the world seems to overshadow the good, especially with the epic 2020 quarantined addition of life. It's almost impossible to protect that space. I mean, can you truly choose who walks down the street with you or who comes in the library. In this instance, my advice to you is to see the good and to focus on the things in your life that you are grateful for.

THE SPACE BESIDE ME:

If you are single, you have major and complete control of the space directly around you. If you are married or live with family, while space is yours, there are limitations. This space is the space where you select who can and who won't be in your space. A single person can decide who exactly can come into their home and enter their space. In saying this, understand that this is where we choose who has access to our peace, I mean space. The level of goodness or toxicity is brought to your space by invitation only, and you are holding the party. This means we should examine our spaces and see if the levels of stress and defeat we are experiencing is based on who we've invited into our space. Bad relationships, toxic friendships, and horrible tribe choices cause contention and unrest in your space. However, when the tribe you have around you is one that is positive, loving, encouraging, and prayerful - you can't lose.

God is in the midst of a group, especially whose mind is focused on Him. So make sure that everyone in your tribe is on the same page of purpose and greatness as you are. This will make sure that y'all protect and preserve one another's peace; I mean space.

THE SPACE INSIDE OF ME:

Your heart, mind, and soul are all inside you; I would dare to call these components your peace.

The Bible states, *"And the peace of God, which surpasses all understanding, will guard your hearts and your minds in Christ Jesus."* (Phil 4:7)

When we guard our space within, we keep our minds on Jesus and consistently pray and thank God no matter what state we are in, knowing that it could have gone another way. God could have allowed the worst to happen to us, and instead, it all works out for the good. So, we have to guard our hearts and minds against our negative thoughts and keep our minds on Christ. He needs to be our space. If we have Jesus at the center of our space, then we have it all. And God will keep every other area in order.

Journal Entry #14

What is in your global space? (space you can't control?)

_____
_____
_____

What or who is in the space beside you? (people and places that you choose to be in your space?) How does those people, places, or things contribute to your peace?

_____
_____
_____

For all of the toxic people places or things in your life, what is your personal solution to fixing your space(peace) for healthy outcomes in your life?

_____
_____
_____

How will you protect the space inside of you? It starts with putting God first?

_____
_____
_____

Protect your space, that's all you have.

DAY 15

COVENANTS – FRIEND OR FOE?

Covenants are important; the right connections or agreements can move you to your next position in every area of your life. A covenant is an agreement between you and God, someone else, or a group of people. We often talked about the covenants we make with God and how it pushes us to do more and become more.

That's a great place to start...with God! I gave God my life so many years ago, which has caused me to live a certain way. I cannot pretend like I hit the mark all the time, and most times, I didn't hit it the first time, but I strive daily to hit it. Sometimes I beat myself up because I am far from where I want to be, but God is a loving patient, and He waits for me. God is waiting for you to make a covenant with Him, as well.

Covenant with people...

Well, no man is an island. I am the first person who, when something does not appear to be going the way I need it to, I will take it back from the person assigned and do it myself. I am learning and getting slightly better with that. God is faithful and He is always working on me. I am blessed that God has given me a tribe of people in my life who are very special to me and they let me know when I am doing the most. I thank God for my husband, who holds my main covenant. When he first came into my life, I saw his greatness, and I love it. But y'all...my husband would challenge me, offer me his insight and wisdom, and I fought it initially because it's hard to see things from a different perspective when you birthed it, but his perspective has grown up and matured me. I am so grateful for Him and his patience with me. Secondly, my tribe are my sisters from another mother who have been with me through the years. We have a life covenant; we have challenged each other, shared in each other's pain, supported each other, and have been each other's strength. Guess what we are all better women for being a part of each other's lives. My family, the "Bowens" family, there are too many words even to express this covenant. We did not choose each other, but God handpicked and put us all together and made a covenant with Himself for us to serve Him. These people have been my best friends through the good, bad, and the ugly. They have been honest with me, prayed for me, and if I had to choose my family, I would not change one person. These people are my entire life.

Covenant with yourself...

You must make a covenant with yourself. A covenant to love yourself, to forgive yourself, and to extend grace to yourself. You must make a covenant to do better and to take time to care for yourself. You must make a covenant with yourself to be your best and to do your best despite all the things you may face in your life. Commit to finish what you started and to reach for your dreams.

The Foes...

Let us also be very clear about our inner circle and make sure that they are no foe. When your heart is so big, sometimes you can't see the tares in the wheat. Friends who pose as foes, the reality is that we have to be careful. Now, I do not subscribe to cutting people off and just being away angry. I subscribe to forgiving people and letting them go live their lives in a way that best suits them but has no effect or defect in my life. That does not mean we don't love them. It simply means their part in the book is over. And that's Ok. Take inventory of who is around and be sure that they are not spoiling your work, dreams, goals, and vision. And if you aren't sure, don't share - you can't afford to let anyone mess up your dreams.

The Bible says, in Numbers 30:2, *"If a man makes a vow to the LORD or swears an oath to obligate himself by a pledge, he must not break his word; he must do everything he has promised."*

Promise yourself to keep your covenant with God, yourself, your family, and your treasured friends. Don't turn back, and if there needs to be a change I any of your vows to honor, grow, and progress to where you would like to be, update the vow, and keep it. You are worth it.

Journal Entry #15

What does the term "covenant" mean to you?

_____

_____

_____

_____

What vows do you need to make to yourself?

_____

_____

_____

_____

For all of the toxic people places or things in your life, what is your personal solution to fixing your space(peace) for healthy outcomes in your life?

_____

_____

_____

How will you protect the space inside of you? It starts with putting God first?

_____

_____

_____

Make the vow to yourself and keep it!

DAY 16

A LIL' MORE COURAGE, PLEASE...

Courage is a big word, seven letters, the word rage living inside of it as the motor pushing it. It takes courage to continue to get up each time you are knocked down. It takes courage when things don't go as you plan them. Sometimes, if we're honest, it may take some rage to keep you pushing forward. It takes courage to choose something different from the status quo. It takes courage to parent a child alone. It takes courage to work three jobs to feed your family. It takes courage to go to school one class by one class until you attend graduation - 10 years later. Courage is doing it, AFRAID!!!

Yes...Life is scary and the things that we are faced with every day are very frightening, sometimes you have to ask God to give you just a little more courage. God will do just that. He will place you at tables in front of your known enemies and you will have the victorious outcome. Now, sitting across from enemies can be extremely uncomfortable but take courage because God is faithful. God will not put you in a position to fail, and sometimes when we think things aren't going our way, we think it's a fail, no. It's a moment to learn from the experience so that we don't make the error again or do it better the next time.

The immature us would say, "Why would God put me in a position to fail?"

The mature us would say, "God, what lesson am I to gain from this experience?"

Please don't think that I am saying you don't feel the fear, anxiety, or craziness for one second. Feel it!!! The cold hard pain of the uncertainty and then take courage, do it anyway. Move forward anyway, step out on faith anyway. Go after it anyway. Know that what is there in front of you is there and then do it anyway. I know it sounds repetitious, but sometimes you just have to hear, read, and see it over and over again so that you can remember it.

Courage means following your heart. It means making hard choices, changing jobs, ending a friendship, and sometimes moving away. It means sacrificing what is safe for what can be life-changing. That's scary - because sometimes the fear of the unknown can be scary - take courage, take heart, and do it anyway. You have to broaden your horizons and expand your circles so that you have opportunities to do something different presents itself. You will be surprised by these opportunities, and it will change your life, experiences by experience.

The Bible says, in Acts 27:25, *"Take courage! For I believe God. It will be just as he said."*

Friends...It will be just what GOD said for your life!!!

Journal Entry #16

Write the list of things you need to take courage with (Cross them out as you conquer them):

_____

_____

_____

_____

_____

_____

_____

_____

_____

_____

_____

_____

_____

_____

_____

_____

_____

Acts 27:25, "Take courage! For I believe God. It will be just as he said."

DAY 17

MISUNDERSTOOD!

Hi, my name is Priscilla Danielle, and I am the picture of misunderstood, welcome!

Since a child, I have always felt different. I would see everyone doing something one way, and I couldn't do it. I had to do it my way. I see everyone wearing or desiring the same things, but I had to have my individual style. If a project or report was done, I always had to add more to it. And I would get the extra points and the teachers' happy responses, but the students were brutal. I often heard and still hear sometimes. she does too much, she just has to add glitter, she just had to make it, or best her just has to be different. I apologized and minimized myself for so many years because of this. So, I went inward, and it closed me up; I would only share what I am comfortable with. I even found that I would do just the minimum as I got to high school with my schoolwork, and it played out even in college until I dealt with it. Amazingly, what others think is harmful banter can really hurt and scar someone that's sensitive and change the course of their lives.

I thank God because my difference made the difference in who I as a woman today. I relish in my difference, and I embrace them, and I don't know what regular is or how to do. It's not the way I see things. Everything has glitter to me; everything has the ability to shine and be better. Everybody has a gold mine in, and the gold mine in me will always call forth the goldmine in someone else. God birthed us all by design and with the purpose, aka goldmine. The love of God is what heals those wounds and when we submit to God, and He begins to tell you who you are with scriptures like:

Jer. 1:5, *"Before I formed you in the womb I knew you before you were born I set you apart; I appointed you as a prophet to the nations."*

Psalms 139:14, *"I will praise thee; for I am **fearfully and wonderfully made**: marvelous are thy works; **and** that my soul knoweth right well."*

Romans 12:2 *"And be not conformed to this world: but be ye transformed by the renewing of your mind, that ye may prove what is that good, and acceptable, and perfect, will of God."*

These are all powerful verses that remind me of my space and calling here in the world, and I share them with you. Embrace being misunderstood by people because God understands. God created for somebody, and as you go through life, you will begin to meet these people, some for a moment and some for a lifetime, but you will know that you were born to meet them, impact, and grow for the connection. Being misunderstood is not all bad; sometimes, it's just GREAT.

Journal Entry #17

What areas in life do you believe you are misunderstood?

_____

_____

_____

Are these areas places where you find yourself protecting and not sharing?

_____

_____

_____

How can you use these areas within your visions and dreams in order to progress? How can it help you become closer to God with these differences?

_____

_____

"Father show my friend that their difference is Your glory being manifested in their lives. Show them that it is truly a blessing and not a curse. Father help them to embrace their creativity, their vision, and their purpose. Let them know that while others may misunderstand You, You are fearfully and wonderfully made them in Your image, and they are called for this time and season. In Jesus' Name, Amen"

DAY 18

GOD IS THE KEEPER OF THE DREAM...

Life distracts you sometimes, and we find ourselves far from the dream or far from where we expected to be. We find ourselves irritated with ourselves because we are not where we expected to be. But God is the keeper of the dream.

Last night I had a dream, and the dream was a dream I'd been having with my eyes wide open - I would daydream about it. However, it's something about a dream when your sleeping. It seems real; the feeling and the presence is real. So, the dream I had last night I had been waiting on for quite some time. It's the way God lets me know it's time to end a thing or to begin. I forgot about parts of the dream, but God reminded me that he is the keeper of our dream, so all the needed parts will show up.

Don't worry, sometimes it seems like we missed it, or the time for the dreams we had has passed. If the dream was given to you by God, it will come to pass. Don't get discouraged while waiting; keep building, journaling, and writing the vision. Some people have one dream others have many. I say write it all down because it will come true. And if you are writing the details while you are waiting when it comes forth, you will be more than ready.

I was simply sent to remind you to dream again and write it down because it matters when the time is right and the people who are present when the dream becomes a reality. See, sometimes it's not our fault that the dream did not come alive yet, it had to wait for the people the dream was sent to reach, and if they had an arrival delay, then your dream may be delayed. Fret not because we all heard it before, delayed is not denied!!! So, keep the dream alive by talking about (with those you trust), writing about it, planning toward, and consistently praying for it, and it will come.

When was the last time you dreamed a dream of your future?

_____

_____

_____

_____

_____

_____

_____

If you dreamed the same dream multiple times, what was different in this dream than the other dreams?

_____
_____
_____
_____
_____
_____
_____
_____
_____

What steps can you take now to lay the groundwork for when it's time to put the dream into a plan and a plan into action.

_____
_____
_____
_____
_____
_____
_____
_____

Day 19

WRITE FOR YOUR LIFE...

The reason I wrote this journal was that writing has helped my life in such a major way. It has been my outlet when I'm happy, planning, sad, angry, depressed, and overjoyed. Writing has been my way out of the darkness. I discovered that writing was a safe place for me because I am an introvert, and I live with my thoughts and self-talk, which can be very vicious, so writing was and is my relief. This body of work was produced because writing is power.

This year I started writing what I desired for my life. It seemed I was just jotting things down. A few years ago, I looked back at what I wrote and noticed that I reached every goal on the list. I noticed that God made it all happen. I noticed that my mind was more focused on the goals that I wrote. I noticed that writing caused me to expound and go further in my thoughts and desires, so when it came time to produce what was written, I would have a place to draw from.

The Bible says in Habakkuk 2:2-3, "*2 And the Lord answered me, and said, Write the vision, and make it plain upon tables, that he may run that readeth it."*

3 For the vision is yet for an appointed time, but at the end, it shall speak, and not lie: though it tarry, wait for it; because it will surely come, it will not tarry."

That's the covenant that God made with us, that if we write the vision and make it plain, He will do it. I always thought this was a scripture until I realized the things I wrote came true. If you give yourself and your dreams a fighting chance for no other reason, write for your life. The world needs you and what's inside of you, and some time to write it may not only save your life but the lives of others.

Journal Entry # 19

What's in your heart that needs to be remembered? (Here is your opportunity to lay it all out for yourself.)

Day 20

MAKE MANIFEST

Put all of it into action; this journal has had you writing and thinking, more importantly, provoking your future. All of the thoughts, ideas, and possibilities are endless. I've said it; the future belongs to you. I beg to differ-right now belongs to you. What are you going to do with this book full of hopes and dreams; this is the part where you change your future. This is the part where you do it afraid; this is where you put your money where your mouth is. This is where you step out on faith, knowing that God has your back, front, and sides completely covered. It will come forth. MAKE MANIFEST!

The vision is here; it's time to awake from the dream and put it in motion. It is time to do the research, start designing, and make business cards. Also, it's time to sign up for classes, time to take seminars, time to arrange Zoom for your meetings. Exhaust Google--dig, dig, and dig until you find all the information you need to start.

Listen, I can tell you that I was afraid that it wasn't perfect every time I started something new, and it may have even flopped. But I did it over and over again until it worked. You have to start somewhere. Now that it's on paper take the next step, do a mock-up of what the business may look like. Write the outline to the book, then for each chapter, put a description, then write a little every day. YouTube is your friend, there are so many ways to do one thing, and YouTube has information from scared people who started somewhere, and now they are helping you. If you want to fix your credit, do the research or reach out to an agency for help or support. If you said you want to own a home, do the research in your area, some agencies will help you and sometimes give you money, but you have to dig. The information does not come to you; you go to it and pull it out.

The Bible says in Psalms 42:7, *"deep calleth unto the deep."*

The information you seek will come as you look for it. I know confusing, but I swear it seems if I am not looking, I can't find anything, but it opens right up the moment I go seeking. Seek it out so that you can manifest what you desire. MAKE MANIFEST...produce it, display it, demonstrate, and bring it to life. Breathe into your vision and dreams get to work.

Journal #20

At this point, it's all about doing. Take the next 30 days and get three things that started in your dreams:

1)_____

_____
_____
_____
_____

2)_____

_____
_____
_____
_____

3)_____

_____
_____
_____

Take this next 30 days to pour your heart soul and time into your first project, whatever it may be, and see what you have then keep going. The next 30 days after that...do the next 3 steps. It's a process and you got this. MAKE MANIFEST!!! PRODUCE!!!

DAY 21

THE FINISHER

The Bible says in Philippians 1:6, *"being confident of this very thing that he which hath begun a good work in you will perform it until the day of Jesus Christ."*

You will finish what you've started. Here's why...If you reach the end of this journal, I have finished what I thought I could never obtain. I am who this book was written for.

There was a long time that I felt like I was not good enough, and so I would become easily discouraged by my thoughts of fear and lack of faith in myself. Even bigger, I lacked faith in God. This journal is everything I have used in my life to help me complete this journal.

Now, I pass this journal to you, and I assure you that you are good enough with all of my heart. You are better than good; you are great. Greatness is all over you and your children and your children's children. God did not let you pick up this journal by accident. It was written just for you. What you have inside of you is necessary and needed, don't talk yourself out of it. Someone is waiting to receive what you have to give; you have to get it out there. You have to reach the people they need. Whatever the gift or the dream, it will impact someone else's life in a way that will change their trajectory and ultimately put them on a path to reach their very own expected place in life.

With hands raised, I submit that it was me. I was born for your adversity, and all the trials and errors I faced in my life have been poured into this body of work. So, I charge you to be a finisher! With tears in my eyes and joy in my heart, I believe that we have collided at the exact perfect time for you to do some amazing things on this earth so, may God be with you as He is with me.

Journal #21

Use this space to write a prayer and verse that you desire to carry with you on the journey to completion:

_____
_____
_____
_____
_____
_____
_____
_____
_____
_____
_____

MY VERSE:

Beloved, I wish above all things that thou mayest prosper and be in health, even as thy soul prospereth. 3 John 1:2

MY PRAYER FOR YOU:

"Dear Heavenly Father, I pray for every friend that has read this book and has made strides to heal, free themselves, and run toward their dreams. Father give them grace and

wisdom for the next parts of their journey. Remind them to write the visions and the words that You reveal in their lives. I pray that the anointing to finish what they've started to be upon them now. Father, let Your grace be upon them and Your peace within them and Your progress overshadowing their lives. Thank You, Father, for every trial, every error, every single lesson, and growing pain for it has brought us all to this moment. Thank You, Father, for my friends, be with them, bless them, heal, and change their lives.

In Jesus' Name, I pray! Amen."

ABOUT THE AUTHOR

Priscilla Bowens Victor

Priscilla Bowens Victor is the Owner/CEO of Pretti Inc. Not only is she an author, but she is a fashion designer, hairstylist, and make-up artist. Priscilla was born and raised in Philadelphia, PA.

She is a wife and a mother of three boys. Priscilla has been writing for many years, spending most of her time journaling and writing poetry. While she has been a lifelong writer, she is publishing her first journal, and she welcomes you along for the journey. The most important thing to her is helping people achieve their goals and believe in their dreams, and that this can happen by writing it all down.

www.ingramcontent.com/pod-product-compliance
Lightning Source LLC
Chambersburg PA
CBHW071506070526
44578CB00001B/459